This is a tale that has been told
Round Wearside hearths since days of old
I know not if the tale be true
I leave conclusions up to you.
'Tis said the story doth begin
With Robert Hylton's wicked sin.

The Cauld Lad of Hylton

a traditional tale

Illustrated by Joan Henderson

for
Caron, Paula and Sue

published by Newcastle upon Tyne
City Libraries & Arts.

Illustrations
© Joan Henderson, 1990

Calligraphy
© Madeleine Dinkel, 1990

※

The Cauld Lad of Hylton
is based on an original poem by
T. Arthur
with additional verses by
Bill West

※

ISBN 0 902653 93 8

published by Newcastle upon Tyne
City Libraries & Arts.

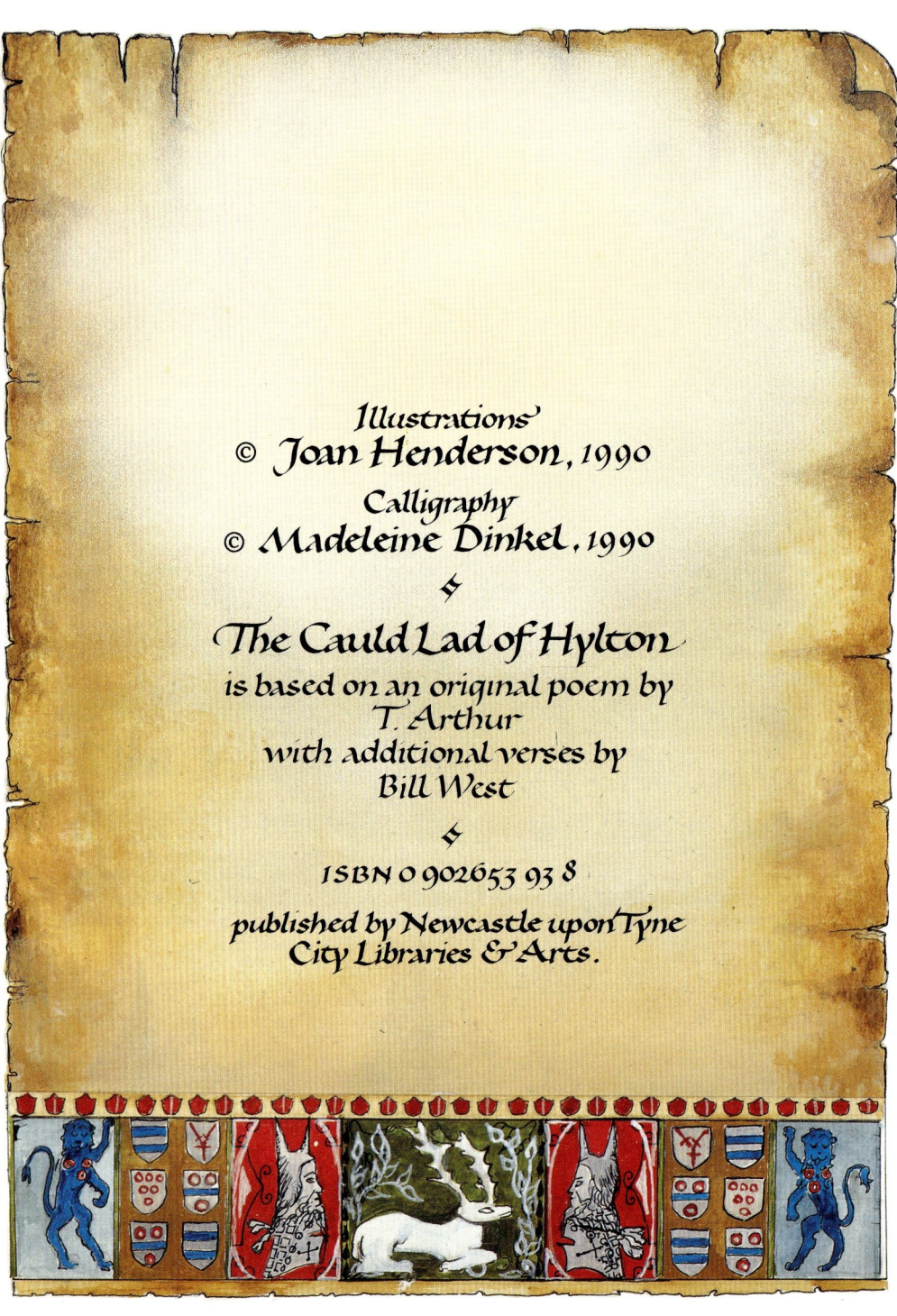

And when night's gloom o'erspread the world, The groom all silent stood,

All pale within the castle hall
Save where he dropped with blood.

Oft in the hall or on the road
The murdered lad is seen

Walking about with head in hand
Of horrid ghastly mien.

And round the spacious castle walls
He walks with heavy tread,
Singing the strain in accents clear
From the gory, trunkless head.

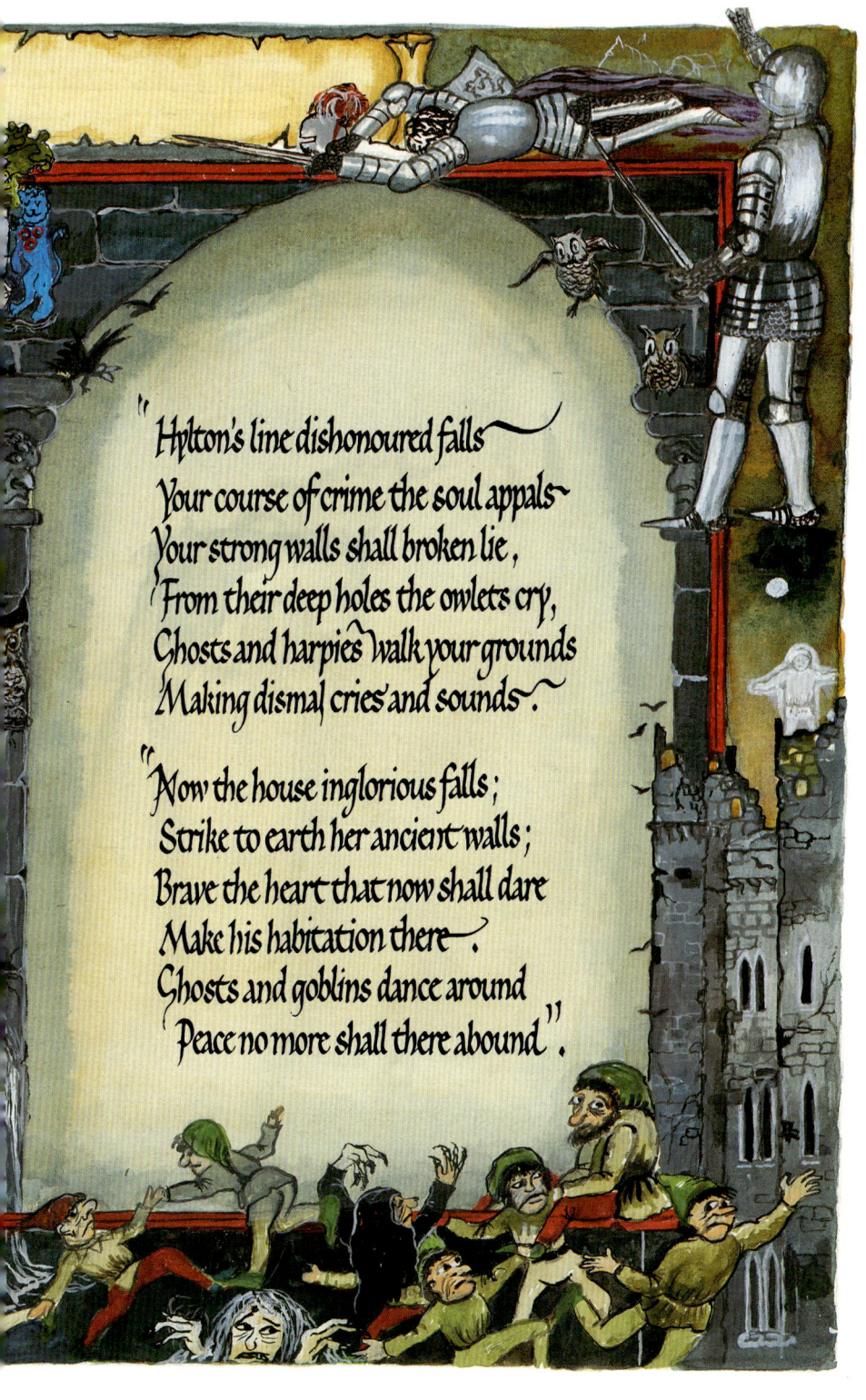

Soon as the servants are in bed
He to the kitchen flies;
And then they hear him at his pranks
And hear his solemn cries.

Should he refuse, to middle stream
Again he pulls the boat,
And taking off his comic head
He then demands a groat.

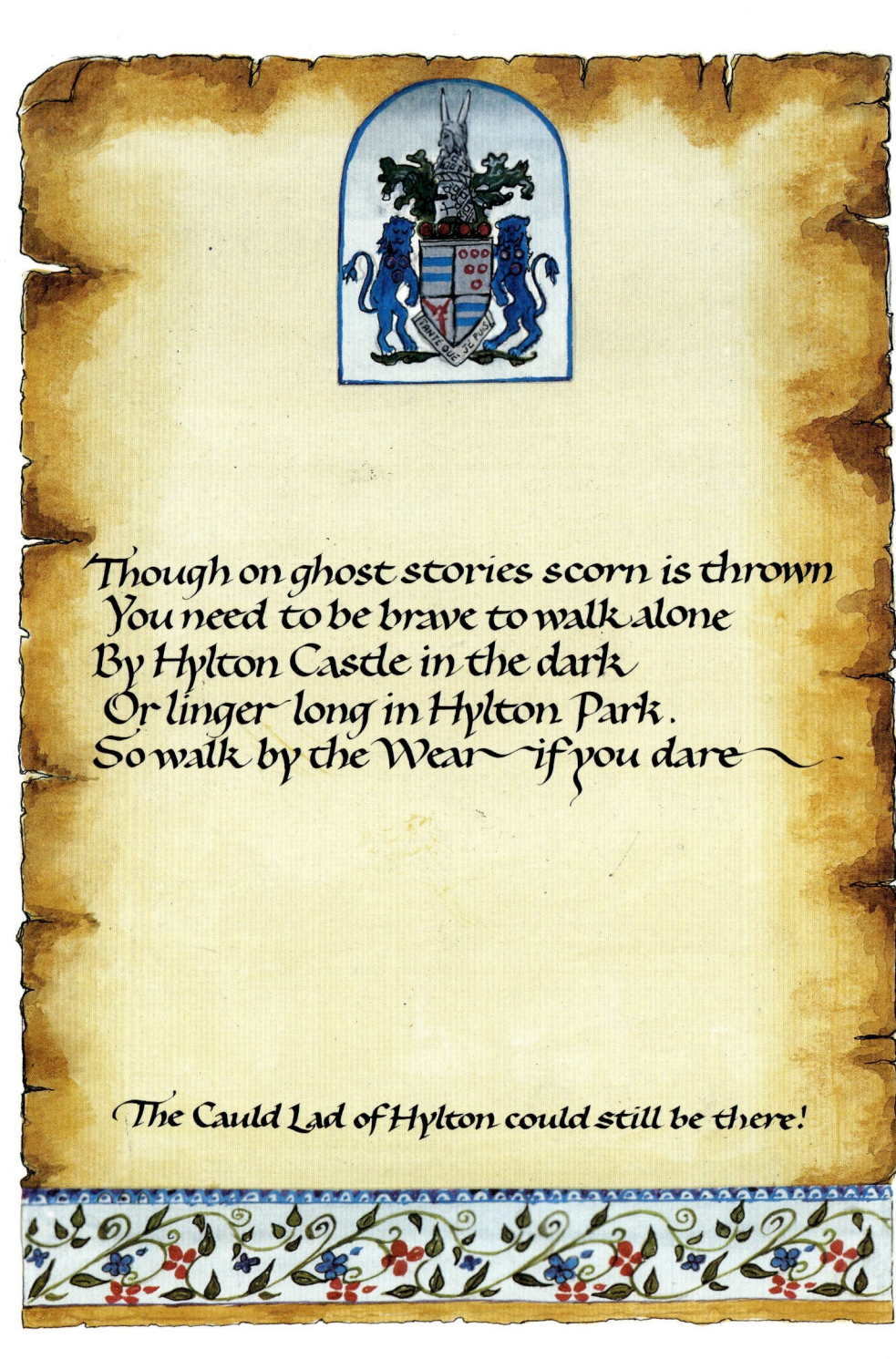